*The World in*

# The World in Tune

Elizabeth Gray Vining

Published by
PENDLE HILL PUBLICATIONS
WALLINGFORD, PENNSYLVANIA

THE WORLD IN TUNE

*Copyright, 1942, 1952, 1954, by Elizabeth Gray Vining*

*First published in association with* PENDLE HILL *by*
HARPER & ROW PUBLISHERS *1954*

*Reprinted by* PENDLE HILL *1968, 1994*

*For information address Pendle Hill Publications,*
*Wallingford, Pennsylvania 19086-6099*

Acknowledgment is made to the following publishers and individuals who have granted permission for the reprinting of copyrighted material from the books listed below:

BARNES & NOBLE, INC. for "Before Sleep" from *Mediaeval Latin Lyrics* (1929) by Helen Waddell (also permission of Constable & Company, Ltd. and Helen Waddell).

JONATHAN CAPE, LTD. and Mrs. H. M. Davies for "Sweet Chance" from *The Collected Poems of W. H. Davies.*

HOUGHTON MIFFLIN COMPANY for "The Monk in the Kitchen" from *Rose of the Wind* by Anna Hempstead Branch, copyright, 1938, by Ethel Lyman and Henry W. Lyman.

THE MACMILLAN COMPANY for "Pater Noster" from *Kings and the Moon* by James Stephens, copyright, 1938, by The Macmillan Company, and "Little Things" from *Collected Poems* by James Stephens, copyright, 1926, by The Macmillan Company (also permission of Macmillan & Company of Canada, Mrs. James Stephens, and St. Martin's Press, Inc.); lines from *Stray Birds* by Rabindranath Tagore (also permission of Macmillan & Co. of Canada, the trustees of Rabindranath Tagore, and St. Martin's Press, Inc.) ; "Into the Twilight" from *Collected Poems* by W. B. Yeats, (also permission of Macmillan & Co. of Canada, Mrs. W. B. Yeats, and A. P. Watt and Son); passage on Meister Eckhart from *The Flowering of Mysticism* by Rufus Jones.

CHARLES SCRIBNER'S SONS for "Sonnet III" from *Poems* by George Santayana, copyright, 1923, by Charles Scribner's Sons, 1951, by George Santayana.

THE VIKING PRESS, INC. for the passage from *Embezzled Heaven* by Franz Werfel, copyright, 1940, by The Viking Press, Inc.

COVER ART: Stained-glass quatrefoil Austrian (Ebreichsdorf, near Wiener Neustadt), ca. 1380 from The Cloisters Collection, 1936, Acc. # 36.39.2. Used with permission of The Metropolitan Museum of Art, New York, New York.

*Library of Congress catalog card number 54-9007*

*Printed in the United States of America by*
*Thomson-Shore Printing Company, Dexter, Michigan*
*August 1968: 2,000*

*April 1994: 2,000*

*Prayer is the world in tune.*

HENRY VAUGHAN

Most of the essays in this book were originally included in two pamphlets, *Anthology with Comments* and *World in Tune*, published in 1942 and 1952 respectively by Pendle Hill. To them have been added an essay first written for the *Tsuda Reader*, in Japan, and an essay and poem previously published in *TheFriend*, Philadelphia.

Pendle Hill is a Quaker center for advanced religious and social study, a place of work and worship, an experiment in community, situated at Wallingford, Pennsylvania. To it come students, often with their families, to engage in a common search for solutions to fundamental problems of life and thought in today's world. Besides the autumn, winter, and spring residential terms, the activities of Pendle Hill include short summer programs, personal retreats, conferences, lectures, short courses and institutes, and a series of pamphlets— Tracts for the Times— and books. Among the best-known and loved pamphlets have been

Howard Brinton's *Guide to Quaker Practice,*
Bradford Smith's *Dear Gift of Life,* and William
Taber's *Four Doors to Meeting for Worship.*

PENDLE HILL PUBLICATIONS COMMITTEE

8

## INTRODUCTION

Some books never grow old. This little book by Elizabeth Vining is one of them. For some of us who have known the joy of her presence as well as her writings, *The World in Tune* portrays many rich facets of her life: her sensitivity to beauty in nature, in poetry and in the writings of the saints. She writes as she lives, responding with her whole being—mind, body and spirit—to beauty.

This openness to glory and wonder "implies a faith that the gift of God will come to the prepared soul." She admits that when she was in college faith was defined "as believing something you know is not true"—that it was just wishful thinking. It took her "many years of living to know faith as a basis of action." In 1942 when this book was printed, she lamented that "the age of faith is admittedly past," that the scientific materialism and psychological insights into self had largely taken the place of faith and intuitive insight. Today there is greater humility about scientific truth being the only valid one; there is greater credence in an imaginative intuition behind their scientific discoveries which defies description but comes in many forms of truth. Even in today's world with all of its violence and cruelty, many men and women of faith believe there is a mighty leaven that "leaveneth the lump," that all is not lost, and that despair of the darkness only seasons the pervasiveness of the leaven.

One discovers a joyous optimism in Elizabeth Vining's writings. She has little time for sober sides, though the soul's time of darkness she fully understands. Joy came in her own life not only in the "minor ecstacies" that lifted her heart, but from a level and quality of Being that is their eternal source. Even when the inner Light burned low, "cramped heart knew again the happiness that is of the universe, not of itself and its possessions." This same source of Light and Truth lies in every path. Its discovery needs only the seeing eye and the open heart from which can come not only personal faith and joy but compassions and action in a suffering world. As Blake once said "Joy and pain are woven fine."

After too few years of a happy marriage Elizabeth Vining's husband was killed in an automobile accident. She was seriously injured. Her references to death and how to face it are among the richest examples of faith in this book. "Somehow we must learn not only to meet it (death) with courage, which is comparatively easy, but to bear it with serenity, which is more difficult, being not a single act but a way of living." She quotes a pasage from William Penn's *Some Fruits of Solitude* in connection with his meeting with the death of his beloved wife Guilielma Springett Penn: "Sorrow cannot be fought and overcome; it cannot be loaded or escaped; it must be lived with." Elizabeth Vining adds, "sorrow is for the inward side, joy for the outward," quoting Aubrey de Vere:

> Grief should be
> Like joy, majestic, equable, sedate;
> Confirming, cleansing, raising, making free;
> Strong to consume small troubles; to command
> Great thoughts, grave thoughts, thoughts lasting
>     to the end.

Elizabeth Vining is a Christian and a Quaker. Personal prayer and communion with God and intercessory prayer for others have been a strong part of her inner life. Her spirit has been warmed by the writings of the mystics and various saints from every generation. She knows that behind the words both spoken and written

11

which mark the distinctions of people of various faiths lie inner experiences that have transformed their lives.

As a devotional book to dip into many times over, this little book cannot be surpassed. It might well "speak to your condition" whatever that happens to be.

DOROTHY M. STEERE

*The World in Tune*

## PREPARATIONS

Yet if his Majesty, our sovereign lord,
Should of his own accord
Friendly himself invite,
And say, "I'll be your guest tomorrow night,"
How should we stir ourselves, call and command
All hands to work! "Let no man idle stand!

"Set me fine Spanish tables in the hall;
See they be fitted all;
Let there be room to eat
And order taken that there want no meat.
See every sconce and candlestick made bright,
That without tapers they may give a light.

"Look to the presence: a.e the carpets spread,
The dazie o'er the head,
The cushions in the chairs,
And all the candles lighted on the stairs?
Perfume the chambers, and in any case
Let each man give attendance in his place!"

Thus, if a king were coming, would we do;
And 'twere good reason too;
For 'tis a duteous thing
To show all honor to an earthly king,

And after all our travail and our cost,
So he be pleased, to think no labour lost.

But at the coming of the King of Heaven
All's set at six and seven;
We wallow in our sin,
Christ cannot find a chamber in the inn.
We entertain Him always like a stranger,
And, as at first, still lodge Him in the manger.

Christ Church Manuscript

WHAT A PICTURE this anonymous poet paints of seventeenth-century preparations: the hustle and bustle in the hall, which was still the center and heart of the manor house, the fine Spanish tables with their fittings, the candlesticks polished so that they gave light even without tapers, the carpets and the cushions, the candles on the stairs, and the fragrant herbs in the bedrooms; and most important of all, the gladness of the service and its generosity, counting no cost, "so he be pleased." And then in contrast, the poet shows us the slovenliness and indifference with which we receive spiritual visitation.

The earthly king, it is true, gave warning of his visit, while the King of Heaven gives no hint beforehand. Preparation for the Spirit must be continual and alert. Meister Eckhart, the great German practical mystic of the fourteenth century, said, "We must ever be prepared for the gift of God and ever newly," and long before that Jesus of Nazareth, the greatest mystic of all and the most practical, told us how to prepare. "Watch and pray, for ye know not when . . ."

Preparations for spiritual visitation, then, consist not in silver polishing and setting up fine Spanish tables, but in watching and praying, in maintaining an attitude of "alert passivity," of quiet awareness, and in arranging one's outward life so that it does not interfere with such inward activities. Such preparations imply a faith that the gift of God will come to the prepared soul, even though no messenger arrives with the word: "I'll be your guest tomorrow night."

Today the Age of Faith is admittedly past. The number of people who are able to assert, and to prove their assertion by their transformed lives and shining faces, that they have actually been visited by the Spirit, is small. Thomas Kelly was such a one, and the power of his influence is due to the fact that he was

17

authentically one of these rather than to what he wrote and said. There are undoubtedly many more people who have had the experience but who are not willing to talk about it, whether from reserve or uncertainty or because they use different symbols. The quality of their work and their lives, however, is such that we declare almost involuntarily that they must have had some vitalizing spiritual experience.

If these luminous authentics are few in the modern scene, there are nevertheless increasing numbers of intelligent and thoughtful people who are willing to enter upon preparation and spiritual training, even though many of them prefer to describe it in psychological rather than religious terms. These are the people who are returning from the arid regions of skepticism and belief in scientific materialism; they are listening instead to the new scientists like Dr. Albert Einstein, Sir James Jeans, and Sir Arthur Eddington, who find a spiritual force in the universe, though they may not call it God. Many thoughtful moderns are impatient or perhaps even afraid of religious symbols, but they have experienced the stillness within themselves and received intimations of its source. Often they have even learned to depend on it and to seek to deepen and widen it. Explicitly or implicitly they agree with Pascal when he said, "Thou wouldest not have sought me if thou hadst not already found me."

It may be that in such preparations as these, made quietly and secretly and sometimes more in venture than in faith, the King of Heaven is Himself taking a hand.

I wrote these notes on preparations for a royal visit a good many years ago, having not the remotest idea that I should ever find myself preparing to entertain as a house guest, if not a king at any rate a crown prince, and not once but twice, in Japan and again, three years later, in the suburbs of Philadelphia. Experience shows me that the seventeenth-century poet has not exaggerated the amount of "stirring" that is done in preparation for the coming of royalty. And if there are in the twentieth century fewer people to give attendance in their places within the house, there are countless people outside who did not figure in the earlier scene: the representatives of the press, the radio, and television!

O World, thou choosest not the better part!
It is not wisdom to be only wise
And on the inward vision close the eyes,
But it is wisdom to believe the heart.
Columbus found a world and had no chart
Save one that faith deciphered in the skies;
To trust the soul's invincible surmise
Was all his science, and his only art.
Our knowledge is a torch of smoky pine,
That lights the pathway but one step ahead
Across a void of mystery and dread.
Bid then the tender light of faith to shine
By which alone the mortal heart is led
Unto the thinking of the thought divine.

GEORGE SANTAYANA

WHEN I WAS in college, we had little use for faith, which we defined as "believing something that you know is not true." When someone quoted from that respected but seldom read piece of ancient literature, the Bible, "Faith is the substance of things hoped for," we said, glibly knowledgeable, "Oh, yes, wishful thinking." The *Concise Oxford Dictionary's* definition, "spiritual apprehension of divine truth apart from proof," made no sense at all to members of the course in "General Philos." who were learning to "question everything; accept nothing without proof." It has taken me more than fifteen years of living to know faith as the basis of action.

Without faith, faith in a book of directions, faith in oneself, faith in another's word, written or spoken, faith in "the soul's invincible surmise," nothing, not even the simplest thing, would be done. From the child who takes a first step to the scientist who spends years in the laboratory testing and proving the hypothesis he or she has set up, all creative action is based on faith. The higher and nobler the object or force on which one sets one's faith, the more daring and effective the action.

"O ye of little faith!" Jesus so often cried despairingly to his disciples. It was not their intellectual beliefs that He was concerned about, but their paralyzing failure to apprehend the truth that walked beside them. As they learned to use and trust and act upon their little faith, it grew stronger.

Franz Werfel, in his fine novel *Embezzled Heaven,* set forth his own ideas about faith through the conversation of two of his characters.

"I myself," I said after a while, "have at very rare moments, which are not my worst ones, a strong inclination to faith—even to faith in the strictest sense—"

"Inclination!" she laughed with a touch of mockery. "It is like an inclination to be a singer. A person can possess a voice. That is a gift which comes from Heaven. But what are you going to do with your voice if you do not study and practice and work hard, without allowing yourself a single day's remission? Faith too is an art that must be studied and practised and practised and studied, like singing."

THREE HUNDRED and sixteen years ago a little girl struggled alone with a fundamental problem of prayer. Ready-made prayers did not satisfy her. She wondered if it was right to use prayers written by someone else to express another's need. In trembling rebellion she made up her own prayer, and wrote it down. For some time she used it every morning, a good prayer for a twelve-year-old, honest, modest, yet determined: "Lord, thou commandedst the Israelites to offer a morning sacrifice, so I offer up the sacrifice of prayer and desire to be preserved this day." Later she discovered that a prayer need not be written at all, not even by herself, and she felt that at last she had learned true communion with God.

This anxious, sensitive, and adventurous child was Mary Proude, who grew up to marry first Sir William Springett, a Puritan in Cromwell's army, and, after his early death, Isaac Penington. Together they became Quakers in the earliest days of the Society, and Isaac Penington's mystical writings helped to determine the nature of Quaker thought and practice. Mary Penington's daughter, Gulielma Springett, married young William Penn.

At the time when little Mary Proude was writing her own prayers, George Fox, then unknown to her and born in the same year, already knew that his "words should be few and savoury, seasoned with grace." At the opposite pole from these obscure children, was the fashionable divine of the day, John Donne, the famous dean of St. Paul's. Crowds flocked to hear his learned sermons, into which he poured the beauty and passion that had once gone into his secular poems. His prayers also were exquisite pieces of writing, composed not only with a literary regard for beauty of phrase and cadence, but with a courtier's feeling for formal and reverent approach. In one long prayer he wrote, "I beseech thee that since by thy grace I have thus long meditated upon thee and spoken of thee, I may now speak to thee." For "sudden, inconsidered, irreverent prayers" he had no use, and averred that "God will scarce hearken" to such. How scandalized he would have been if he had known of St. Teresa, less than a century earlier, sitting on a river's brim and informing God that the reason He had so few friends was that He treated those He had so badly!

In spite of Donne, however, the tide was turning against set prayers. Milton found them a "supercilious tyranny." Most Protestant sects discarded them, though few so thoroughly as the Quakers. Prayer was often offered in Friends' meetings for worship, but always extemporaneously, under the promptings of the Spirit, and it was seldom written down afterward. William Penn said of George Fox, "The most awful, living, reverent frame I ever felt or beheld . . . was his in prayer." But no collection of George Fox's prayers was made for later generations.

The mystical writers who see the spiritual life as a ladder assign the prayer of prepared words to the lower rungs. Meditation, contemplation, the prayer of quiet, the prayer of union are later stages. Yet periods of aridity come to all, even the saints, when meditation is empty and unreal or even distasteful, the mind wanders, the heart is earth-bound, and spontaneous prayer is difficult or even impossible. Then verbal prayer becomes a support for the flagging spirit, a frame for our vague and reluctant reaching toward God. The old prayers, beautiful and true, composed by people who have understood the struggle and found victory, used over and over by praying hearts, have acquired a sort of patina. They speak to God, and also to us, disciplining our irresolution, informing our imagination, directing our will, inducing a reverent awareness from without, when the inner doors appear to be closed or lost.

We can read them, as Père de Caussade taught us to do all our spiritual reading, slowly, savoring each phrase or sentence, following all the lines of thought it suggests, waiting till each line is exhausted before going on to the next. Or we can memorize them, to recall in the times when books are not available, in wakeful periods in the night, while waiting for a train, or as a means of centering down in Meeting when distractions scatter our thoughts. A phrase may accompany us through the day, flashing through our routine tasks, arising to soften a human contact that might turn thorny, steadying us in time of anxiety or stress, or expressing a sudden joy.

The prayers in this book have come from various sources, some old, some recent, and with them are some of the lines of thought that they have suggested to one familiar with the lower rungs of the ladder.

It is a good thing to give thanks unto the Lord
and to sing praises unto thy name, O most highest;
    To tell of thy loving-kindness early in the morning,
and of thy truth in the night season.

PSALM 92: 1-2

❦

OUR FIRST thought in the morning and the last at night should be of God, whether we express it, as the Psalmist goes on to recommend, "upon a loud instrument" or in the secret recesses of our hearts, in the sensitive twilight period between sleeping and waking.

When first thy eyes unveil, give thy soul leave
To do the like; our Bodies but forerun
The spirit's duty; True hearts spread and heave
Unto their God, as flowers do to the sun.
    Give Him thy first thoughts then; so shalt
      thou keep
    Him company all day, and in him sleep.

So in "The Morning Watch" Henry Vaughan pictures all life turning toward God at dawn.

27

The rising winds
And falling springs,
Birds, beasts, all things
Adore Him in their kinds.
  Thus all is hurl'd
In sacred Hymnes and Order, the great Chime
And symphony of nature.   Prayer is
  The world in tune.

It seems to be of the nature of religion—of all religions—to turn in the morning, after the darkness and oblivion of the night, to the source of returning light.  I remember one morning, in a little inn in Japan, looking down from my window into an inner garden. I saw an old man in a cotton kimono standing before a little Shinto shrine, a small replica, with its weathered wooden sides and crossbeams pointing upward on the roof, of the great shrines of the Sun Goddess at Ise. He bowed low, clapped his hands three times, stood for a few moments in silence, bowed again, and then went back into the house, his wooden clogs scraping lightly on the dirt path winding among the gray rocks and broad-leaved evergreens of the little green garden. I don't know which of the myriad Shinto deities was summoned to attention by the clapping of his

It is a natural sequence that the Psalmist suggests to us in the 92nd Psalm. We are aware in the morning of God's loving-kindness, of God's gift of the new day, fresh and unspoiled, of the opportunities that lie before us. At night, when we are older by twelve or fifteen hours of experience and wiser for our knowledge of failures and incompletely realized opportunities, then it is God's truth that is uppermost in our minds. But whatever our disappointment and fatigue—or it may be, our satisfaction and hope—if we have kept "Him company all the day" then we can most completely give ourselves into God's hands for the night and "in him sleep."

Helen Waddell, author of *The Desert Fathers* and other scholarly and fascinating books, has translated into verse some of the Christian Latin Lyrics, and among them the following poem by Prudentius, the fourth-century Spaniard who held a high place at court and retired to devote himself to religion.

### BEFORE SLEEP

The toil of day is ebbing,
    The quiet comes again,
In slumber deep relaxing,
    The limbs of tired men.

And minds with anguish shaken
 And spirits racked with grief
The cup of all forgetting
 Have drunk and found relief.

The still Lethean waters
 Now steal through every vein,
And men no more remember
 The meaning of their pain.

Let, let the weary body
 Lie sunk in slumber deep;
The heart shall still remember
 Christ in its very sleep.

Sweet Chance, that led my steps abroad
Beyond the town where wild flowers grow—
A rainbow and a cuckoo, Lord!
How rich and great the times are now!
Know, all ye sheep
And cows that keep
On staring that I stand so long
In grass that's wet from heavy rain—
A rainbow and a cuckoo's song
May never come together again;
May never come
This side the tomb!

W. H. Davies

ONLY A FEW people, and those few but
infrequently, know ecstasy. It is a big
word; it means a state of being outside oneself
and outside time, caught up in an overwhelming
emotion; it implies a high occasion and a
greatness of response to it. Mystics have used
the word to express the ineffable joy of union
with Reality, the flight, in Plotinus' phrase, of

the alone to the Alone; it applies to the selfless raptures of human love and parenthood, to what artists feel when what they create seems to be coming through them from something beyond. With such grandeurs of experience, alps towering above the plain of daily living, I am not now concerned. I am thinking of what I have learned to call minor ecstasies, bits of star dust which are for all of us, however monotonous our days and cramped our lives, however limited our opportunities.

Everyone has these moments, more or less often, according as they are recognized and cherished. Something seen, something heard, something felt, flashes upon one with a bright freshness, and the heart, tired or sick or sad or merely indifferent, stirs and lifts in answer. Different things do it for different people, but the result is the same: that fleeting instant when we lose ourselves in joy and wonder. It is minor because it is slight and so soon gone; it is an ecstasy because there is an impersonal quality in the vivid thrust of happiness we feel, and because the stir lingers in the memory. Fragments of beauty and truth lie in every path; they need only the seeing eye and the receptive spirit to become the stuff of authentic minor ecstasies.

The poets, who have high and noble words for the great experiences of the soul, know well these smaller ones too. W. H. Davies saw a rainbow and heard a cuckoo call in the same moment, and the combination made him cry out, "How rich and great the times are now!" Marvell's soul, delighted with the fruit and flowers in a garden, "glided into the boughs," and

> There like a bird it sits and sings
> Then whets and combs its silver wings.

Wordsworth's heart "with pleasure fills and dances with the daffodils." Most of the fugitive descriptive verse that comes and goes through our newspapers and magazines probably has its source in minor ecstasies.

I well remember the first one that I recognized and consciously put away in my mind as a child hoards the birthday pearl to make a necklace. I was fifteen, and it was August in Cape May. Because the land comes down in a point between the ocean on the east and the wide and apparently shoreless bay on the west, the sun there sets over the water. We liked for that reason to walk on the boardwalk after dinner. The western sky one evening was filled with flame and molten gold, and gold and flame shone in all the moving facets of the water. Behind us the eastern sky was pearly; into it the moon rose, spilling pale silver over the gray-blue sea. Even as I caught my breath at the lovely drama of the contrast, an airplane, a great silver bird more rare and wonderful then than now, came suddenly out of the heart of the sunset, sailed above the long, lonely beach, and flew deep into the moonlight. My young heart bounded against my ribs like a bird in a cage, and memory has held that scene for me in colors as bright and soft as those in which I first saw it. Ever since, that memory has been for me a sort of yardstick; if what I see or hear makes me feel at all as that made me feel, then it is a minor ecstasy.

There have been countless others down the years: crape myrtle flashing through the slanting silver of a sudden southern downpour; the flute passages in Beethoven's Fourth Symphony; the cold curve of the river in winter where it turns between purple wooded banks; shared laughter over nothing more than fundamental understanding; the call of a cuckoo above the peat bogs in Skye; the whistle of a cardinal in the dark of a suburban February morning; the smell of wet wood and seaweed at a ferry wharf; the fragrance of sun-warmed honeysuckle on stone walls.

Once when for long months sorrow had clamped tight my heart, it was a minor ecstasy that showed me that life might again hold joy for me. I woke in the morning to the sound, I thought, of rain on the porch roof, but when I opened my eyes I saw that it was not raindrops making that soft and playful patter but locust blossoms falling from the tree above. For a fleeting second my cramped and stiff heart knew again the happiness that is of the universe and not of itself and its possessions, and like Sara Teasdale, when in similar circumstances she heard the wood thrush through the dusk, "I snatched life back against my breast, and kissed it, scars and all."

It is well to recognize and cherish the moments when they come; it is an added joy consciously to collect them. The collector's instinct is strong in everyone, and a hoard of minor ecstasies brings more keen and lasting pleasure than all the autographs and little china jugs in the world. It costs but a notebook and the time it takes to jot down the few words that bring them vividly back to us when time has overlaid them in our minds with dust, not of stars, but of the erosion of daily life.

Writing them down saves them for us. It reminds us in the blank periods that come to all that we have had these moments in the past and will have them again. It shows us what kind of stimuli most often rouse them so that we can put ourselves in the way of them again. If it is music and not plays, mountains rather than the sea, or contact with people more than either, then how foolish of us not to turn our steps, in so far as we are able, where those things lie.

"Things prized," wrote Thomas Traherne many years ago, "are enjoyed." Writing them down, treasuring them, not only makes our enjoyment keener, it makes us more aware of them, less likely to let them pass unnoticed through sloth or indifference. It serves to polish up the lens through which we see the world about us. Exercising our faculty for minor ecstasies may actually increase the number of them we feel, though we must be careful not to let the lust for collecting cloud our honesty with ourselves. Pretty descriptions in a notebook are worthless; unless there has been that genuine though slight release and lift, that stir and even leap of the heart, "like kidlings blythe and merry," it is no ecstasy at all but only a calm appreciation of an admirable scene or sound, or a sparkle from physical well-being.

Now when the walls of the world we have known seem to be tottering above our heads, when bleak winds from a hidden future go howling past our naked ears, when the familiar treasures that have kept our safe lives snug seem to be dimming and receding, still a collection of minor ecstasies can be a source of joy, secret, inviolable, inexhaustible. The time in which we live calls on us for great emotions, sorrow for all suffering people as well as whatever tragedy and frustration we as individuals may have to meet; it calls on us for vision and dedication, for sacrifice, for courage; it calls on us also not to despise the day of small things. Great moments we shall have, with their blinding light of revelation, but they will be comparatively rare. There will be many more stretches of dimness and dusk when we plod along in faith and determination. Minor ecstasies will light these gray stretches like faint but unmistakable stars, if we but look for them.

Who would have thought my shrivelled heart
Could have recovered greenness?  It was gone
Quite underground as flowers depart
To feed their mother-root when they are blown;
        Where they together
        Through the hard weather,
Dead to the world, keep house unknown.

These are thy wonders, Lord of Power,
Killing and quickening, bringing down to hell
And up to heaven, in an hour;
Making a chiming of a passing-bell.
        We say amiss,
        This or that is:
Thy word is all, if we could spell.

And now in age I bud again;
After so many deaths I live and write;
I once more smell the dew and rain,
And relish versing: O my only Light,
        It cannot be
        That I am he
On whom thy tempests fell all night!

GEORGE HERBERT

As George Herbert was only forty when he died, and a year or two younger than that when he wrote these lines, his feeling of age must have been due to weariness and inner struggle, and, probably, to illness. A mystic, he perhaps wrote, too, of the dark night of the soul, that arid and bleak time, experienced by most of the saints, when the Spirit seems to withdraw its presence, leaving the human soul in doubt and despair without its guiding light. A modern writer, Gerald Bullett, has suggested that this dark night of the soul is the well-known human experience of reaction after so intense a striving toward heaven, but the great mystics, unendowed with a psychological vocabulary, have in general described it as the necessary stage before the soul laboriously climbing the Ladder of Perfection "dares the final bound" and reaches union with the divine.

Whether he writes of the dark night of the soul or of a more common alternation of mood, how wonderfully Herbert expresses the refreshment of greenness after aridity, the budding of the shrivelled heart, the smell of dew and rain, and how human and endearing is his renewed relish of versing. "I live and write," he says, as if the two were inseparable—as, indeed, for some people they are. In his somewhat limited field of writing, George Herbert occasionally achieved perfection, but even for those whose finished works always seem

> Like the empty words of a dream
> Remembered on waking,

if they are born with the desire to write, the *cacoëthes scribendi,* living and writing are two parts of the same whole.

Short prayer pierceth Heaven.

THE CLOUD OF UNKNOWING

❧⸱ᘒᘐ⸱❧

BRIEF PRAYERS, sometimes called aspirations, often arise out of our daily life, not merely in time of danger and crisis, when even the determinedly skeptical find themselves crying out for help, but in our most peaceful times, if we follow William Penn's advice and make a practice of stepping home, within ourselves, at intervals. Such prayer, St. Francis de Sales assures us, may be "interwoven with all our business and occupations without hindering them in the slightest degree," and he likens it to a traveler pausing on a journey for the moment's refreshment that will enable him or her to go forward the better.

Many of the great practicers of prayer have included some of these "short but ardent efforts of the heart" in their written works, from which they can be culled for our use. It is much better, as St. Francis says in his

*Introduction to the Devout Life,* for us to make our own aspirations prompted by our own needs and the motions of our hearts, but one of the characteristics of periods of dryness is that we do not then spontaneously reach out toward God. Then it may be helpful to choose another's aspiration that expresses what we would like to feel, and carry it in our minds during the day.

O my God, why dost thou ever remember me whilst I, alas, so often forget thee?

St. Francis de Sales

I will hear what the Lord God will Speak.

Psalm 85:8

My God, behold me wholly thine; Lord, make me according to thy heart.

Brother Lawrence

Help me, O Lord God, in my good resolution and in your holy service. Grant me now, this very day, to begin perfectly, for thus far I have done nothing.

Imitation of Christ

O Lord, make clean my heart within me.

PSALM 51: 10

O Holy Spirit, descend plentifully into my heart; enlighten the dark corners of this neglected dwelling and scatter there thy cheerful beams.

ST. AUGUSTINE

## LITTLE THINGS

Little things that run and quail,
And die, in silence and despair!

Little things that fight and fail,
And fall, on sea and earth and air!

All trapped and frightened little things,
The mouse, the coney, hear our prayer!

As we forgive those done to us,
—The lamb, the linnet, and the hare—

Forgive us all our trespasses,
Little creatures, everywhere!

JAMES STEPHENS

JAMES STEPHENS' tenderness and under-standing for the small animals whose exist-ence is hidden and precarious reminds one of William Blake's earlier and angrier lines:

44

A Robin Redbreast in a Cage
Puts all Heaven in a Rage.
Each outcry of the hunted Hare
A fibre from the Brain does tear.

I have heard, just once, the outcry from the hunted hare. In that case, it was a half-grown rabbit which Hamish, my little West Highland terrier, started on the Wissahickon. We were walking along the dirt road beside that clear green stream on one of those early spring days when the air is full of tinkle and gleam of icicles melting from purple rocks, and the hollows in the woods are still rustling with dead leaves, when the sun warms the cedar's bright green, and the shadows of the bare tulip trees and gray beeches are thin and ethereal. I did not see the bunny; I only saw Hamish suddenly galvanized into a swift white streak kicking up leaves from the ditch behind him. When he was almost on his quarry, the little creature doubled on its tracks, gave a scream so shrill and so packed with terror that it sounded nearly human, and raced between the dog's legs toward me. A human cry that is nearly animal in its abandonment to pain and fright and an animal cry that is almost human in its intensity and awareness, are alike shocking and harrowing. Hamish doubled back too, and I lunged at him as he came past me, but he was too quick. He caught the little creature, gave it one joyful shake, and then looked up, puzzled and disappointed because it could run no more. He meant no harm; he was only following his instincts. The horror for me lay not so much in that small, limp, furry body, deprived of the life that had been so vivid in it, as in the outcry that came not from its pain but from its fear. The memory of it lingers to hurt, as if it had indeed torn a fiber from the brain.

Blake and, in a lesser and unacknowledged degree, James Stephens are both mystics. It is part of the make-up of mystics that they feel a sympathy and a union with animals. It is the gift of both Blake and Stephens as poets that they can pass along this feeling in words so pointed and so touching that they communicate the experience to others, who have not felt it themselves, or, having felt it, have not given it recognition.

### PRAISE OF CREATED THINGS

Be Thou praised, my Lord, with all Thy creatures,
  above all Brother Sun,
    who gives the day and lightens us therewith.


And he is beautiful and radiant with great
  splendor,
    of Thee, Most High, he bears similitude.


Be Thou praised, my Lord, of Sister Moon and
  the stars,
    in the heaven hast Thou formed them,
      clear and precious and comely.


Be Thou praised, my Lord, of Brother Wind,
    and of the air and the cloud and of fair
      and all weather,
    by the which Thou givest Thy creatures
      sustenance.

Be Thou praised, my Lord, of Sister Water,
    which is much useful and humble and
      precious and pure.

Be Thou praised, my Lord, of Brother Fire,
  by which Thou has lightened the night,
    and he is beautiful and joyful and robust
      and strong.


Be Thou praised, my Lord, of our Sister Mother
  Earth,
    which sustains and hath us in rule,
    and produces divers fruits with colored
      flowers and herbs.


Be Thou praised, my Lord, of those who
  pardon for Thy  love
    and endure sickness and tribulations.


Blessed are they who will endure it in peace
  for by Thee, Most High, they shall be
    crowned.


Be Thou praised, my Lord, of our Sister
  Bodily Death
    from whom no man living may escape.
    Woe to those who die in mortal sin:


Blessed are they who are found in Thy most
  holy will,
    for the second death shall not work them
      ill.

Praise ye and bless my Lord and give Him
   thanks,
      and serve Him with great humility.

St. Francis

❧❧❧

St. Francis' "Hymn of Praise of Created
Things" is familiar, especially the lines
which speak of Sister Water and Sister Bodily
Death. It is a lovely thing, with its exquisite and
precise phrases and its dramatic contrasts of
awe and tenderness, of gentleness and power,
Brother Sun and Sister Moon, Sister Water and
Brother Fire. It is even more moving in its
recognition of the beauty in the universe, its
realization of our kinship with all its
manifestations, and its simple acceptance and
thankfulness to the Reality that is through
and behind and above it all.

Those who tend to think of religion as long-
faced, dour, self-torturing and inhibited, must
surely feel the ground slipping out from under
their feet when they encounter St. Francis of
Assisi. Volumes have been written about him,

his place in medieval life and thought, and his influence on art, literature, and the church, but none has given us more vivid flashes of his personality and his spirit, his tenderness and gaiety, his feeling of kinship with all life, than the fourteenth-century *Little Flowers of St. Francis* and *The Mirror of Perfection,* two of the most delightful and most endearing of books on the spiritual life. What if much of them be legend? Legend is sometimes truer than fact.

In art, both medieval and modern, St. Francis of Assisi is generally pictured surrounded by birds flying, perching on his shoulders, or walking on the ground at his feet. His sisters the birds were dear to him indeed; they enter again and again into the story of his life. Many times he said he would like to have a law made that no one should take or kill sister lark or do her any harm, and that every year on Christmas Day people should throw wheat and other grains to the birds. The lark was his favorite, for she had a cowl like a religious, wore humble brown clothes and sang sweetly in the heavens, praising God; but he loved them all.

One of the most beloved of the *Little Flowers* is that which tells of his preaching to the birds. "My little sisters, the birds," he began, "much are ye beholden to God your creator." While he spoke, they opened their beaks and spread their wings and stretched out their necks, a whole multitude of them in a field, and reverently bowed their heads to the ground, showing thus the joy that St. Francis' words gave them. He walked among them, touching them with the hem of his garment, and not one stirred. When he had finished his sermon, made the sign of the cross over them and given them leave to depart, they soared up into the air with wondrous songs and divided themselves into four parts, like a cross, and flew away north, east, south, and west, singing praises to God (and perhaps also to St. Francis) as they went.

Then there is the story of the wild turtle doves that St. Francis rescued from a youth who was taking them to market. After chiding them gently for allowing themselves to be caught, St. Francis built nests for them, so that they could lay their eggs and raise their young, which they did. They abode tamely with the friars and never went away till St. Francis gave them leave with his blessing. As for the youth who trapped them, he became a friar and served the order with great holiness.

Larks and swallows and turtle doves were not the only birds St. Francis knew: he had also a falcon for a friend. When he was praying in his leafy cell on the mount of La Verna, before he received the stigmata, a falcon who had built her nest nearby "dwelt familiarly with him." Every night a little before matins, she would sing loudly and beat her wings against his cell, until he woke up and rose for his orisons. "And when," the story tells us, "St. Francis was more weary at one time than another, or more sick, or more feeble, this falcon, after the manner of a discreet and compassionate person, sang later."

The medieval attitude toward falcons makes this story the more poignant. The great sport of the Middle Ages was falconry. Great lords and knights and ladies kept their favorite falcons always with them, hooded, on their fists or on perches above their beds at night and behind their chairs at dinner. Many a great bishop kept his on a perch in the abbey cloisters. There was an elaborate ritual, etiquette, science, and vocabulary of falconry. The birds had their trainers and attendants, their mews where they were kept while moulting, their wardrobe of hoods and jesses and little silver bells, the best of which were made at Milan, one of each pair a semitone higher than the other. They had their hierarchy. A gerfalcon belonged to a king, a peregrine falcon to an earl, a merlin to a lady, a sparhawk to a priest, a goshawk to a yeoman. The falcon was no humble, religious lark; she was a proud and fashionable bird of prey—and St. Francis was one of God's poor little ones. Their friendship, in the medieval scene, had a special piquancy and flavor.

God's Troubadour they have called St. Francis of Assisi, because he had in his youth some skill in the secular art and because he himself thought of all the servants of God, and especially the Friars Minor, as minstrels. "For what," he said, "are the servants of the Lord but his minstrels who should raise the hearts of men and move them to spiritual joy." He reproved a friar who showed a sad and troubled face to the world, telling him to keep his sorrow between the Lord and himself and study always to show joy before others. His own ever-springing joy expressed itself not only in his tenderness and delight in all created beings but sometimes also in the special forms of the troubadours of France. One of the most charming passages in *The Mirror of Perfection* tells us:

For the most sweet melody of spirit boiling up within him frequently broke out in French speech and the veins of murmuring which he heard secretly with his ears broke forth into French-like rejoicing. And sometimes he picked up a branch from the earth and laying it on his left arm he drew in his right hand another stick like a bow over it, as if on a viol or other instrument, and making fitting gestures sang with it in French unto the Lord Jesus Christ.

St. Francis of Assisi was not the only saint who read "Blessed are the meek" in the French way: "Blessed are the debonaire." There are, for instance, enough stories of St. Teresa and St. Rose of Lima, who also had the gift of gaiety, to give some basis to the assertion: "The good are always merry"; but in St. Francis' life, more than any other I know about, the stream ran not only humble and precious and pure, but joyful as well.

O God, unto whom all hearts are open, all desires known, and from whom no secrets are hid, cleanse the thoughts of our hearts by the inspiration of thy Holy Spirit, that we may perfectly love thee and worthily magnify thy Holy Name, through Christ our Lord. Amen.

THIS PRAYER, known as the Purity Collect, is one of the oldest and most beloved prayers of the Episcopal *Book of Common Prayer*. Down through the centuries it has been used in the preface to the communion service, preparing people's hearts for the gift of the divine presence and, indeed, expressing in its few and luminous words the essence of worship.

It is ascribed to the learned Englishman of the eighth century, Alcuin, who included it in his Votive Mass for Invoking the Grace of the Holy Spirit, but he may well have taken it from some still older group of prayers. Alcuin, churchman, scholar, and philosopher, was summoned at the age of fifty to Charlemagne's court from the Cathedral of York, where his life had been lived and from whence his fame had gone forth. Out of his immense enthusiasm for learning, for teaching, and for libraries, came that revival of learning on the continent of Europe which foreshadowed and perhaps made possible the later and more splendid glories of the Renaissance. Only one of his achievements was his sacramentary, or missal, based on the Gregorian sacramentary of Rome with masses and prayers from Gallican and other sources.

Four centuries later his prayer appeared in *Sarum Missal,* the first English prayer book in which the various "uses" were gathered together into a uniform service book—English because though it was written in Latin it was used in England. Osmund, the nephew of William the Conqueror and bishop of Sarum, built a cathedral in the shadow of the royal castle of Old Sarum and compiled the manual of prayers revising and combining the old rituals. Circulated in manuscript form, for the use of the priests, not the people, it was in constant use for nearly five hundred years.

His prayer book lasted longer than his cathedral. By 1220 the Norman soldiers had got a bit above themselves, as occupation forces will, and were harassing the priests and hindering them in their duties, to the annoyance of the townsfolk. A new modern city was being built on the plain below. The people all moved down, and they put through the building of a new cathedral with so much vigor and determination that alone of English cathedrals Salisbury is all of a single period.

I remember well a spring visit to the ruins of Old Sarum. We left the city of Salisbury with its spire, its pilgrim's inn, and its shops filled with the coronation mugs of that year, and walked up the long hill to the northeast of the city. The clear chilly wind of early May swept across Salisbury Plain. Some stunted flinty ruins, deep grassy ditches, and high grassy banks were all that was left of the moats and walls, the castle in the Inner Bailey, the town in the Outer Bailey, and the cathedral that Osmund built. Britons, Romans, Saxons, Normans had come and gone. It had the mysterious emptiness and sadness of all abandoned places. The offending soldiers had left no trace, but the prayers that came out of Old Sarum kept its name alive.

By 1350 the anonymous author of *The Cloud of Unknowing* was prefacing his classic treatise on the contemplative life with the Purity Collect, translated into the English of his day:

> God, unto whom all hearts be open and unto whom all will speaketh, and unto whom no privy thing is hid, I beseech thee so far to cleanse the intent of mine heart with the unspeakable gift of thy grace that I may perfectly love thee and worthily praise thee. Amen.

Two centuries later when King Edward VI was twelve years old, Archbishop Cranmer produced the first English prayer book actually written in English, and the Purity Collect appeared in the form in which we have it now. The *Book of Common Prayer* of 1549 lasted only three years, being criticized like all innovations by extremists on both side, the most curious complaint being that it was "nothing but Christmas games," and it was succeeded by a long line of revisions. But through all the changes of rubric and content, this prayer has proved itself indispensable.

The magic bit in it for me, that makes it glow freshly each time I slip the familiar words through my mind, is the word "inspiration." It is used, of course, in the sense of its Latin derivation, *in-spirare*, "to breathe into," and it suggests what Sir Thomas Browne in *Religio*

*Medici* called "the warm gales and gentle ventilations of the Spirit." The cleansing and airing of our souls by the stirring of God's spirit is not all that is asked for, however; desirable and unspeakably comfortable though that is, it is not to end there. The familiar, the sound, the eternal sequence of inward attitude and outward action follows: "That we may perfectly love thee and worthily magnify thy Holy Name."

The last phrase once seemed to me an outworn formula grown meaningless. Even when one substituted the more modest word, "praise," for the grandiloquent "magnify," how could a grubby and self-absorbed little human add anything worthy to the Name of God? Since I have lived in Japan, however, I see it in another light. In an Oriental country Christians are a conspicuous minority, professing much. They are observed and appraised acutely, not on their words but on their acts, their way of living. By their deeds they not merely cast shame or credit upon their fellow Christians, but they magnify or belittle the God with whose Name they are identified.

But this prayer may go back farther than Alcuin or even his predecessors. In the Shemoneh 'Esreh, the great Jewish prayer of Eighteen Petitions which scholars cannot date exactly but parts of which were used in the earliest days of the Pharisaic synagogue, may be found a plea which expresses even more directly this sequence between pure hearts and worthy acts: "Cleanse our hearts to serve thee in truth."

## The Elixir

Teach me, my God and King,
In all things thee to see,
And what I do in anything,
To do it as for thee.

Not rudely, as a beast
To runne into an action;
But still to make thee prepossest,
And give it his perfection.

A man that looks on glasse
On it may stay his eye;
Or, if he pleaseth, through it passe,
And then the heaven espie.

All may of thee partake:
Nothing can be so mean
Which with his tincture (for thy sake)
Will not grow bright and clean.

A servant with this clause
Makes drudgerie divine:
Who sweeps a room, as for thy laws,
Makes that and th' action fine.

This is the famous stone
That turneth all to gold:
For that which God doth touch and own
Cannot for lesse be told.

GEORGE HERBERT

❧ ❦ ❧

THE PHILOSOPHER'S STONE, which transmuted base metal into gold, was still a serious quest in the seventeenth century, as perhaps it is again, now that we can transmute coal into silk stockings and milk into overcoats. George Herbert here uses that "famous stone" as a symbol for the attitude of mind which invests humdrum daily tasks with color and splendor and value. The secret is in the first stanza: "What I do in anything, to do it as for thee." It is another way of expressing the conviction that all life is a sacrament.

One of the most difficult pieces of drudgery to invest with spiritual grace is the homemaker's job of forever producing laboriously something that is destroyed in a fraction of the time it takes to put it together, and of which the debris must be removed afterward. Hardly are the lunch dishes done before it is time to peel the potatoes for dinner. And tomorrow the same; today's special effort cuts nothing off tomorrow's necessities. The engagement is fought daily but no ground is taken. Penelope's web is forever being unraveled. Rooms must be swept again and again.

There are two schools of thought about housework. The first accepts it as a dull and tiring job and sets about getting it done without repining, sometimes even without interrupting the flow of higher thoughts. Brother Lawrence, the seventeenth-century lay brother in the monastery of the Carmelites Déchaussés in Paris, "had naturally a great aversion" to the work of the kitchen, but he is famous for being able to practice the presence of God there even better than in the set times of meditation in his cell. "The time of business," said he, "does not with me differ from the time of prayer, and in the noise and blatter of my kitchen, where several persons are at the same time calling for different things, I possess God in as great tranquility as if I were upon my knees at the Blessed Sacrament." We are specifically told that he did his work in the kitchen well, but if further evidence is needed we may find it in the fact that he was kept on in the job for fifteen years. It takes, however, a special degree of double consciousness to achieve this two-fold success in meditation and culinary effort. Most of us let the beans burn.

The other school applies the philosopher's stone; it looks upon its work as a sacrament, an action that has sacred meaning in spite of its lowly and repetitious form and that gives expression to the will to praise God; it works with the spirit that makes drudgery divine.

Anna Hempstead Branch's beautiful poem on this subject, "The Monk in the Kitchen," is too long to quote in its entirety, but a fragment shows the philosopher's stone at work:

> Whoever makes a thing more bright,
> He is an angel of all light.
> When I cleanse this earthen floor
> My spirit leaps to see
> Bright garments trailing over it,
> A cleanness made by me.
> Purger of all men's thoughts and ways,
> With labor do I sound Thy praise,
> My work is done for Thee.
> Whoever makes a thing more bright
> He is an angel of all light.
> Therefore, let me spread abroad
> The beautiful cleanness of my God.

This is alchemy at its highest, and at its most successful. Like many other things, it has to work.  Without the real secret, the honest dedication to a Reality honestly believed in, it becomes a process of transmuting grim acceptance into wavering sentimentality, a change of very dubious value.  Honest lead is better than phony brass.

Lord, grant me the sorrow of the humble; a mind escaped from mortal body; to love, to laud, and to behold thee and cherish every act and thought that is toward thee. Grant me a clear and sober and genuinely prayerful mind with real intuition of thy will, together with the love and joy which make it easy to perform. Lord, vouchsafe me always modest progress toward better things, and never to backslide.

MEISTER ECKHART

SOMETIMES WE are repelled by the frenzies of the mystics, by what seem their excesses of other-worldliness, unhygienically kissing lepers, torturing themselves in hideously painful and to us quite unnecessary ways, wishing their families dead that they might give their minds solely to God. Then it is good to turn to Meister Eckhart, who lived in Germany from 1260 to 1327, and who was, according to Rufus Jones, one of the greatest mystics of all Christian history. Of him, Rufus Jones further wrote:

He was a man of sanity, of moral health and vigor, and he had a penetrating humor which is one of the very best signs of sanity and normality. He exhibited religious intuitions of a very high order. He broke a fresh way of life through the jungle of his time and by the depth and power of his personal experience he brought conviction of the reality of God to multitudes of persons in his generation.

In this prayer of his we see his sanity, his moderateness, as well as his pure and lofty spirit. More than most people he had a grasp of that essential flow between the inward and the outward which makes the integrated and effective life. "The active life," he said, "is better than the life of contemplation so far as we actually spend in service the income we derive from contemplation."

To me this prayer is a plea primarily for steadiness and patience. Haste and frothy enthusiasms are to be set aside, and with them the reaction, the fatigues, the loss of pace that can make the spiritual life so difficult a series of ups and downs, of light withdrawn and doubted, of gritty darkness. "Abide courteously and meekly the will of our Lord," says the author of *The Cloud of*

*Unknowing,* "and snatch not overhastily, as it were a greedy greyhound."

The parable of the Sower, as told in Luke, ends with these words: "And that in the good ground, these are such as in an honest and good heart, having heard the word, hold it fast, and bring forth fruit with patience."

Vouchsafe me always modest progress toward better things and never to backslide.

Come, heart, where hill is heaped upon hill,
For there the mystical brotherhood
Of sun and moon and hollow and wood
And river and stream work out their will.

WILLIAM BUTLER YEATS

❧

THE HILLSIDE FIELD was tilted to the morning sun and blazed with orange hawkweed, with the clear yellow of king devil, the white of daisies and yarrow, the rusty blue of prunella, the deep rose of clover. I heard cowbells and the unending, ever-changing hum of insects made up of the buzz of bees, the whizz of a passing fly, the grind of a grasshopper, and the separate busy noises of a hundred others. I heard a song sparrow elaborating his theme, a Maryland yellowthroat simplifying his, a towhee brisk and nasal in the distance. The breeze that lapped the leaves of birches by the stone wall lifted the hair around my face. Suddenly I smelled strawberries, sweet, tangy, wild.

The best berries in my field grew deep in the grass, clusters of bright rubies glistening on a long stem under roughly toothed leaves. Others grew where there was no grass at all, only the carpet of leaves and moss. Some were bedded in the moss as if they had been packed each one separately by a Piccadilly fruiterer. I knelt and picked, planning a supper of fresh asparagus and wild strawberry shortcake, with cream from the cow whose bell I heard in the distance.

My little dog, a West Highland white terrier named Hamish M'Conachie but referred to in the family as His Honor, also liked wild strawberries. He preferred to get them out of my basket, but when that was denied him, he would lie down close to me and bite off the biggest and ripest berries within his reach, snuffling and munching with satisfaction.

As I picked, moving from one patch to another, straightening up to face the breeze and refresh my sight with the long sweep of hills to the southeast, I thought of other wild strawberries hallowed and miraculous in family legend, those that grew beside the road at Loch Earn Head which my sister smelled before she saw them, those soaked in Rhine wine which my father ate in the Black Forest. No others could ever touch those for fragrance or for flavor.

But it was not the flavor or the fragrance that so endeared my wild strawberries to me that I remember now, years later, the touch of the wind as I gathered them, the sound of the insects, the sweep of field and hill. It was the sense I had of nature's largesse, of gifts graciously spread out for my taking, of thankfulness for a delicate pleasure not given by humankind. It was the realization that came slowly seeping into my innermost consciousness of my kinship with all that was, with light and air and earth, with bird and insect and my rough-haired little dog beside me, until I was lifted and freed and lost myself in that which contained and was beyond all these. "Through the grass once again," AE wrote, and I knew it too, "I am bound to the Lord."

Be still, my heart, these great trees are prayers.

RABINDRANATH TAGORE

❦

I THINK I KNOW the very trees that Tagore had in mind when he wrote this, for many of the poems in his volume, *Stray Birds,* were said to have been written at the place in Karuizawa where I spent the summer holidays during my four years in Japan. The house was surrounded by great balsam trees, and the clear pure mountain air was tangy with their fragrance. In the early mornings long shafts of sunlight came slanting through their purplish trunks and green branches, and cuckoos called in the distance. In the hush and the freshness, one's heart was filled with that wonder and awe which come when nature silences us with beauty like a trumpet call. Something more explicit than words, higher than thought, deeper than feeling, seemed to be expressed by those majestic trees, as if they were indeed prayer made visible.

The winter tree
Resembles me
Whose sap lies in its root.
The spring draws nigh;
As it, so I
Shall bud, I hope, and shoot.

THOMAS ELLWOOD

❦

THIS IS very bad poetry, and yet I like it. I like its humility, its hope, and its unconscious humor. It is a refutation of Keats' assertion that beauty is truth, truth beauty, for here in homely and slightly comic guise is an eternal truth. It speaks of the same phenomenon that Herbert describes much more felicitously, the renewal of light after the dark night of the soul, of spring after winter. Only where Herbert wrote joyously of the actuality, Ellwood, chilled, pinched, sapless, is looking forward in a sort of numb faith to the hope of spring.

Thomas Ellwood's poems were long valued in Quaker households. Whittier tell us in *Snowbound* that his family library contained but one volume of poetry and that Ellwood's. A poet himself, he ventured to poke a little fun at his Quaker predecessor:

> And poetry (or good or bad,
> A single book was all we had),
> Where Ellwood's meek, drab-skirted Muse,
>     A stranger to the heathen Nine,
>     Sang, with a somewhat nasal whine,
> The wars of David and the Jews.

It seems a pity for Thomas Ellwood to be thrust aside in this way. If his poetry lacked something, his journal is fascinating reading.

He was the son of Squire Ellwood of Crowell, Oxfordshire, an English Squire of the humorous tradition, red-faced, loud-voiced, domineering, vulnerable in his affections, filled with a determination to do his best—but in his own way—for those he loved. When his son Thomas succumbed to the undesirable doctrines of the Quakers and appeared at dinner with his hat on, the conflict between these two strong personalities was a sort of parody on the deeper and more tragic conflict that was to take place a decade or so later between Admiral Sir William Penn and Son William. Thomas would appear before his father with his hat on, the Squire would angrily snatch it off, Thomas would go for another hat. This stubborn drama continued with increasing frenzy on the Squire's part and entrenched piety on Thomas', until the young man's supply of hats came to an end. Then riding out uncovered, he got an earache and had to submit to roasted raisins applied by his solicitous sister.

In time, after further tribulations and imprisonment in both Newgate and Bridewell, Thomas went to live with the Peningtons at Chalfont St. Peter and put his Oxford education to use in tutoring the children. Gulielma Springett, Mary Penington's daughter by her first marriage, was then a lovely young girl, and Thomas Ellwood obviously fell more deeply in love with her with every breath he drew. None of her large flock of suitors seriously disturbed him till Admiral Penn's brilliant young son appeared on the scene. Then, recognizing that this was indeed "he for whom she was reserved," Thomas relinquished whatever dreams of Guli he had permitted himself, sensibly married his second choice, and settled down to farming and writing third-rate verse, chiefly about Old Testament figures.

One touch of authentic poetry he did have: he was for a time Milton's secretary. That is to say, it was an arrangement for mutual aid; he read aloud to the blind Milton, and the poet corrected his Latin pronunciation and instructed him in rhetoric as they went along. This is why some books say that Milton was his tutor. When the plague of 1665 struck London, Ellwood found a "pretty box" for Milton in Chalfont St. Giles, whither he retreated until London air became safe again. There is a charming tradition that while he was there, Guli Springett used to ride over from Amersham and play the lute and sing to him, but this, I fear, is apocryphal. After Milton had given Ellwood his *Paradise Lost* to read, the former secretary's comment was, "But thou hast said nothing of Paradise found!" And to his dying day, Ellwood believed that the second epic was inspired by his suggestion. Be that as it may, Ellwood wrote a long poem on his friend Milton, in which he uttered a critical comment which has undeservedly been overlooked by the great commentators on Milton. "His natural abilities," wrote Ellwood seriously, "were doubtless of the largest size." To those to whose condition Milton happens not to speak, this devastating praise is precious.

A meek, drab-skirted Muse Ellwood's was perhaps, as his personality was earnest, humorless, and faintly absurd. His good and useful life, rich in love and courage, repeatedly suffered abrupt deflation by the same circumstances that touched others with beauty and with glory. Still there remain those slightly comic, slightly pathetic, but eternally human and valiant lines of his that speak for all of us who, in spite of our numb helplessness in the face of this world's most desolate winter, dare to look forward to a time when we too

Shall bud, I hope, and shoot.

We've seen the cherry blossoms,
We've viewed the harvest moon.
Who dares to say this life
Is not worth living after all?

KUMAGAI NAOYOSHI
(JAPANESE POET, 1783–1862)

SOMETIMES AT NIGHT when I am waiting for
sleep I like to summon up flowers that I
have seen, not single flowers but masses, "ten
thousand at a glance" flinging their beauty so
generously upon the air that they startle and
delight. I like to go back again in imagination
to the place where they bloomed and love over
those enchanted moments. I think of the
different countries I have known and loved
and ask myself which, if I could choose but one
kind of flower, I would cherish from each
country.

The bluebells of England, surely. I was in
Buckinghamshire one May, visiting the places
that William Penn had known. The hawthorn,
about which the English poets have

rhapsodized, had disappointed me a little, perhaps because I had been expecting too much. Then someone said to me, "Have you ever seen a bluebell wood?"

I hadn't, so off I went one afternoon by myself to find one. The directions were enticing: "Cross four stiles and turn to the right." The first stile led me into a field with cows in it; the second had a path that crossed it diagonally, and picnickers were eating canned fruit salad right in the middle of the path; the third field lay high on a hill under the wide sky and there was nothing in it but the wind, and me. When I climbed the fourth stile I saw a path on the right leading down into a beech wood.

The new leaves were small and green and translucent, and the pale sun shining through them made a green light that shimmered like depths of clear water. The ground was blue as far as I could see, pure blue a little deeper than the sky. Thousands of bluebells on their slender stalks swayed a little as the breeze touched them, and it was like ripples on moving water between the aisles of gray beech boles down the hill and as far away into the distance as the eye could reach. Breathless I stood and looked, until heart and mind were filled to the brim with beauty.

In all of America, where there is such variety, I would choose, if I could take but one, the dogwood at Valley Forge. Thousands of trees have been planted over the wind-swept hillsides where the ragged hungry soldiers of Washington's army suffered and endured during that darkest winter of America's struggle for freedom. Now in spring they cover that scene of old suffering with a glory of pink and white blossoms, so breathtakingly beautiful that people come in their thousands to see them, as people swarm to see the cherry blossoms in Japan.

Because of the crowds my sister and I get up early one morning each May and drive to Valley Forge before the rest of the world is stirring. We find no one there but ourselves and perhaps a group of bird enthusiasts who come with binoculars to see warblers as well as dogwood. There is no sound but the chorus of birds, and the long slanting rays of the rising sun touch the hillsides full of blossoms to unearthly loveliness.

In Scotland there is the heather. The hills are rounded and rolling and bare of trees, tumbling over one another like the waves of the sea. In August there comes over them the deep purple mantle of the heather. Bees are busy gathering sweetness for the honey which has its own indescribable flavor and the air is filled with a faint aromatic fragrance, clean and wild. But the greatest glory is the cloud shadows that move across the hills, deepening the color from grape to indigo in ever-changing patterns of shade and movement. I have walked in the Grampian Hills in heather time, and in the Pentland Hills and in the Lammermuirs, and someday I shall go back to Scotland again to see the cloud shadows sailing over the heather.

Of Japan, what should I choose? The cherry blossoms? Certainly I shall never forget the cherry trees in bloom on Momijiyama within the moats and walls of the Imperial Palace, the flowers fuller, more fresh and delicate than those outside and set off by the rosy and pale green buds of the surrounding maples. But we have cherry blossoms here too, gifts from Japan, reflected in the Tidal Basin in Washington and the Schuylkill River in Philadelphia.

The azaleas on the mountain sides above Nikko? They are glorious, but we have azaleas as lovely on the slopes of Grandfather Mountain in North Carolina.

The plum blossoms? Yes, I think of the plum blossoms, the early white ones along the

Tokaido Road when the January air is still as sharp as a knife, or the shell pink and deep rose masses against the thatched roofs of farmhouses on every road leading out of Tokyo, or even the little scraggy tree in the garden of the house where I lived, which used to stretch out a single, sweet-smelling, flower-starred branch in February. I love the plum blossoms, their fragrance and poetry, the symbolism of their courage blooming in the snow.

Yet there is another flower that comes even more poignantly to my mind: the cosmos that in October spread its pink and white blooms and feathery foliage over the scars and ruins of the bombed city. Over the little piles of broken bits of cement, around the shacks made of blackened scrap iron, out of patches of earth at the edge of broken walls it clambered, profuse and gay. It seemed to sow itself; anyone could have it; it spread and spread, covering destruction with beauty. To the plum blossom, the traditional symbol of courage, I would add the cosmos, delicate yet vigorous, spontaneous and hardy, a sign of healing and fresh growth.

Give us grace and strength to persevere. Give us courage and gayety and the quiet mind. Spare to us our friends and soften to us our enemies. Give us the strength to encounter that which is to come, that we may be brave in peril, constant in tribulation, temperate in wrath, and in all changes of fortune, and down to the gates of death, loyal and loving to one another.

ROBERT LOUIS STEVENSON

THE CATHEDRAL of St. Giles in Edinburgh is dim and vast; old battle flags hang tattered and motionless under the vaulted roof. On one side of the nave is the tomb of Argyll; opposite it, that of Montrose—those two who fought each other so bitterly in the religious wars of the seventeenth century and who died in the end on the scaffold. In one corner of the great church is the statue of John Knox, bearded and severe, and across from it a tablet marks the spot from which Jennie Geddes in a burst of religious disapproval flung her footstool at the minister. His offense lay in using the prayer book of 1637, which Archbishop William Laud of Canterbury had rashly prepared for the use of the Church of Scotland.

Everything in St. Giles seems to speak of religion in its harshest and most militant aspects. And then you come upon the Stevenson memorial in a side chapel; a bronze bas-relief of the invalid in his chair, with his afghan over his knees, and beside him the prayer which he wrote. The words, "Give us courage and gayety and the quiet mind," especially, gleam like sunshine in the gray building.

We need the courage that is bravery in peril and constancy in tribulation and something more: courage to stand by what we know to be right, to acknowledge as reasons for our actions the claim of justice or of love. Gayety—but how easily we forget it!—goes hand in hand with courage; it sets to one side the self and its urgencies, and it handles life with a light and healing touch. "To be a joy-bearer and a joy-giver says everything," Mother Janet Stuart wrote, ". . . and if one gives joy to others one is doing God's work." And St. Teresa of Avila was emphatic in her dislike of "sour saints."

Both courage and gayety spring, surely, from the deep, rich soil of the quiet mind. Meister Eckhart's words,

To the quiet mind all things are possible. What is a quiet mind? A quiet mind is one which nothing weighs on, nothing worries, which, free from ties and from all self-seeking, is wholly merged into the will of God and dead as to its own. Such an one can do no deed however small but it is clothed with something of God's power and authority.

Prayers like this of Stevenson's, in which specific virtues are sought, are addressed at least as much to our own deep selves as to God. People have said that such prayers are no more than autosuggestion and they seem to imply that such a label covers and discredits all prayer. But to suggest improvements to ourselves is both honest and humble, and there can be no better or more effective place to do it than in God's presence.

## JUSTUS QUIDEM

Thou art indeed just, Lord, if I contend
With thee; but, Sir, so what I plead is just.
Why do sinners' ways prosper and why must
Disappointment all I endeavour end?
Wert thou my enemy, O thou my friend,
How wouldst thou worse, I wonder, than thou dost
Defeat, thwart me? Oh, the sots and thralls of lust
Do in spare hours more thrive than I that spend,
Sir, life upon thy cause. See, banks and brakes,
Now, leaved how thick! laced they are again
With fretty chervil, look, and fresh wind shakes
Them; birds build—but not I build; no, but strain,
Time's eunuch, and not breed one work that wakes.
Mine, O thou Lord of life, send my roots rain.

GERARD MANLEY HOPKINS

ALDOUS HUXLEY says of this sonnet, "Never, I think, has the just man's complaint against the universe been put more forcibly, worded more tersely and fiercely, than in Hopkins' sonnet." It is, however, a paraphrase of Jeremiah's previous complaint:

Righteous art thou, O Lord, when I plead with thee; yet let me talk with thee of thy judgments: Wherefore doth the way of the wicked prosper? Wherefore are all they happy that deal very treacherously?

Thou hast planted them; yea, they have taken root; they grow; yea, they bring forth fruit; thou art near in their mouth and far from their reins.

JEREMIAH 12:1–2

Though the thought of these two intensely religious men, prophet and poet, is so similar, one fundamental difference has developed in the intervening twenty-five hundred years. Jeremiah in the rest of his chapter goes on to take comfort in the prospect of the Lord's vengeance on his enemies. " 'I will pluck them up from off their land,' saith the Lord, 'pluck them up and destroy them.' " The modern has relinquished the idea of vengeance, but has come into full possession of the ego. *"Mine,"* he says vehemently, "send *my* roots rain."

The answer, as Aldous Huxley pointed out, is to be found in the Book of Job, "that most moving, most magnificent and profoundest poem of antiquity."

Patience is thilke vertu which suffreth debonairely alle the outrages of adversitee and every wikked word.

GEOFFREY CHAUCER

"THE TALE of Melibeus," that excellent but wearying dissertation on pacifism, and "The Parson's Tale" are the only two of the *Canterbury Tales* that Chaucer tells in prose. "The Parson's Tale" is actually a sermon on the seven deadly sins, and is usually skipped even by ardent devotees of Chaucer. As a matter of fact, it contains much that is interesting and even inspiring, as well as some things that are disgusting. The Parson is well known from the Prologue, which everybody reads. His gentleness, his learning, his poverty, his love and concern for his people, his willingness to walk long miles through rain or "thonder" to comfort the sick or the dying, his preaching, and still more significant, his practice of his own precepts have typified for us these five hundred-odd years the ideal country parson.

In his account of the seven deadly sins he is not mealy-mouthed; he gives definite examples of the forms of each sin prevalent in his time, and with them some rather valuable sidelights on social history. He does not limit himself, however, to sins, but describes fully their antidotes among the virtues. It is in this connection that he utters this definition of patience, "which is a remedye agayns Ire."

Patience, as we usually think of it, is anything but debonair. It is a wan, martyred sort of attitude composed of endurance and unshed tears, uncomfortable alike to the possessor and the beholder. In the vocabulary of heads of modern states, who are quick to declare that their patience is almost at an end, it is rage held with difficulty in check, like a bloodhound straining at a leash. In short, patience as we know it today is really impatience. No wonder it is a discredited virtue.

The patience which is debonair (that is, according to the dictionary, characterized by grace and lightheartedness) in meeting outrageous misfortune, injustice, and insult, is something else altogether. No longer negative and pitiable, or angry, it is a fit companion for charm and courage; it sheds its drab garments and wears a scarlet cloak over its heart of gold.

O Lord, who hast taught us that all our doings without charity are nothing worth; send thy Holy Spirit and pour into our hearts that most excellent gift of charity, the very bond of peace and of all virtues, without which whosoever liveth is counted dead before thee. Grant this for thine only Son Jesus Christ's sake. Amen.

☙ ⬥ ❧

In the *Book of Common Prayer* this is the collect for Quinquagesima Sunday, the fiftieth day before Easter. The Epistle reading prescribed for the day is the 13th chapter of I Corinthians, and the collect, which was written new for the 1549 prayer book, is based upon the theme of the Epistle.

"This business of loving!" wrote Vida Scudder in her fine autobiography, *On Journey.* "It isn't simple. 'Thou shalt love the Lord thy God—and thy neighbor as thyself.' Sometimes that paradoxical command has turned me cynic. 'Love may not be constrained by maistrie,' as Chaucer knew."

When you add to love of God and neighbor, love of our enemies, the difficulty becomes acute. "Love," said William Penn soberly, "is the hardest lesson in Christianity; therefore it should be most our care to learn it."

That we love is one of the illusions we moderns most cherish about ourselves. We will admit cheerfully that we are not "strictly" truthful, that we are lazy, greedy, self-indulgent, proud, angry (though we prefer to say righteously indignant), that we take the Lord's name in vain and profane the Sabbath, but all these minor sins, we imply, are amply compensated for by the way we love. "I love people," we say frequently, complacently, and as conventionally as the pious used to boast that they were saved by grace.

Yet obviously we do not love, or the world would not be what it is today. We do not love vividly enough even to avoid conflicts among those who seriously wish to get along together and accomplish good works. Wrangles in committees, acrimonious disputes over the phrasing of resolutions, hard feelings among leaders in women's auxiliaries are only a few items of evidence that even when we are consciously about the Lord's business we do not love. When we encounter people of opposing politics, different races or economic theories, when we meet with opponents who quite openly do not care whether they reach agreement or not so long as they get what they want, our bankruptcy of love proclaims itself in the feuds, persecutions, discriminations, wars, and chaos of our times.

"Love and do what you will," said St. Augustine, but he did not mean, as we seem to interpret it, Pretend to love and be as bad as you want to be. He meant, if you really love, you cannot do ill; all the things that you wish to do, informed by your love, will be beneficent.

Love, powerful, healing, quickening, enduring, the bond of peace and of all virtues, is of God. We cannot constrain it of our own effort, but we can have it as a gift from God, if we want it enough, if we pray for it urgently, unceasingly. Pour it into our hearts in a generous, life-giving flood, for we have sore need of it.

He who comes to do good knocks at the gate;
he who loves finds the door open.

RABINDRANATH TAGORE

THERE IS in increasing use a short, sharp,
contemptuous phrase that disposes of
people who belong in the first category: the
do-gooders, we call them, and sweep them
away as if there were something disgusting or
ludicrous about doing good in the world.
Arrogantly we assume that at best their motive
is primarily the enhancing of their own
satisfaction in themselves, the enjoyment of
that glow which is natural and suitable to the
small child who says, "And I am very happy, for
I know that I've been good." Tagore, I am sure,
did not intend this meaning. If the good we do
is solid and real, if we knock at the gate, laying
aside our condescension and our awareness of
our kind intentions and our good provision,
the gate will be opened.

But love, the love that includes warmth, interest, respect, unselfish desire for others' welfare and growth, willingness to learn from them, encounters no barriers. They melt like ice in the sunshine. The poet's words are true of all our dealings, in the simplest and narrowest meetings between members of the same family, between people and their next-door neighbors. They are true of the relations of one nation with another.

To some, the prayer of intercession is the most natural and congenial way of approaching God. These people find it ungenerous and lonely to enter alone into His presence, and so they would take with them their loved ones, their friends, all the suffering and the needy, the dismayed and the sinning people the world over. They would hold them up in the light of God's love, asking not for specific gifts that might prove cramping or distracting for them, but that God's will be done in their lives. There is far too little of this kind of prayer in the world today, especially too little prayer for our enemies, national even more than personal.

There is so much wrong that needs righting, so little we individually can do, except to pray. That we can always do, and we should not under-estimate the power of prayer. In some way that we do not understand, the very act of selfless prayer seems to open a channel for God's healing action. Evelyn Underhill wrote to a friend in this connection, "Perhaps the prayer we make here may find its fulfillment on the other side of the world. Perhaps the help we are given in a difficult moment came from a praying soul we never knew. It is all a deep mystery, and we should be careful not to lay down hard and fast rules."

In his William Penn lecture of 1950, "And Having Done All, To Stand," Clarence Pickett quoted a prayer for our enemies that came out of sixteenth-century England, which seems to me to be luminous with love and humility and yet not entirely unattainable by our arrogant and hate-filled minds today.

### Prayer for Our Enemies

Merciful and loving Father,
> We beseech Thee most humbly, even with all our hearts to pour out upon our Enemies with bountiful hand, whatsoever things Thou knowest will do them good.

And chiefly a sound and uncorrupt mind wherethrough they may know Thee and love Thee in true charity and with their whole heart, and love us Thy Children *for Thy sake*.

Let not their first hating of us turn to their harm, seeing that we cannot do them good for want of ability.

96

Lord, we desire their amendment *and our own.*
   Separate them not from us by punishing them,
   but join and knit them to us by Thy favorable
   dealing with them.

And seeing that we be all ordained to be citizens
   of one Everlasting City, let us begin to enter
   into that way *here already* by mutual Love which
   *may bring us right forth thither.*

They that love beyond the World cannot be separated by it.

Death cannot kill what never dies.

Nor can Spirits ever be divided that love and live in the same Divine Principle; the Root and Record of their Friendship.

If Absence be not Death, neither is theirs.

Death is but Crossing the World, as Friends do the Seas; They live in one another still.

For they must needs be present, that love and live in that which is Omnipresent.

In this Divine Glass, they see Face to Face; and their Converse if Free, as well as Pure.

This is the Comfort of Friends, that though they may be said to Die, yet their Friendship and Society are, in the best Sense, ever present, because Immortal.

WILLIAM PENN

ENGLISH POETRY is full of beautiful lines about death as the poet faces it for himself. I pull at random out of my memory Donne's "Death, be not proud," Rupert Brooke's "If I should die, think only this of me," Alan Seeger's "I have a rendez-vous with death," Walt Whitman's "Come, lovely and soothing death," Davenant's "Oh, harmless death"; there are many more, defiant, philosophic, meditative, adventurous, full of courage and of beauty.

In comparison, very few poems have been written about death when it strikes those whom we love, a situation that far more urgently calls for the balm and stimulus of beautiful and comforting words. The great elegies impress us more by the skill of their authors than by their understanding of loss. *Lycidas* does indeed contain two lines that throb with genuine grief:

> For Lycidas is dead, dead ere his prime
> Young Lycidas, and hath not left his peer,

but the poem ends with the bubbling up of the young poet's vitality:

> Anon he rose and twitched his mantle blue;
> Tomorrow to fresh woods and pastures new.

Tennyson's *In Memoriam* is full of attempts to universalize his emotions and thoughts about death, but his expression is facile and a little jingly for the modern taste. Matthew Arnold's

*Thyrsis* is too full of the elaborate trappings of the pastoral elegy, too confined by the artificial limits of the form.

Here and there we find short and rather fugitive verses in which the impact of the death of a loved friend has been written down with a freshness and simplicity that almost raises them out of the particular into the universal, as, for instance, some stanzas in the ballads, or Wilfred Gibson's lines on Rupert Brooke. Generally, however, they are too full of the personality of the individual to be of much comfort. Emily Brontë's *Remembrance,* which begins, "Cold in the earth and the deep snow piled above thee," is so packed with the hopeless passion and agony of grief that it is torture to read.

That is why these lines of William Penn's, taken from *Some Fruits of Solitude,* are so valuable. Penn knew whereof he spoke. His beloved wife had died, Gulielma Springett Penn, who has been called the "most fragrant spirit in all Quaker biography." His mother, who like so many mothers of brilliant and sensitive sons, loved and understood him and stood between him and his devoted but impercipient father, had died just on the eve of his great first voyage to Pennsylvania. His son Springett, the only really promising one among his disappointing children, had coughed away his ardent young life at twenty. After a number of years, in which he had come to terms with his sorrow, Penn wrote the lines quoted above. Besides the beauty of their cadence, the preciseness of their words, and the loftiness of their thought, they embody something still more rare and valuable: a calm and utter conviction that what he says is true. He *knows.*

Sorrow cannot be fought and overcome; it cannot be evaded or escaped; it must be lived with. Whether it be sorrow for our own loss or sorrow for the world's pain, we must learn how to shoulder the burden of it, to carry it so that it does not break our stride or sap the strength of those about us through their pity for our woe. Death of the young and vigorous when they still have much to experience and much to give, loss of the rare and precious person in midstream, is comparatively unusual in good times, but in times of war it becomes tragically frequent. Somehow we must learn not only to meet it with courage, which is comparatively easy, but to bear it with serenity, which is more difficult, being not a single act but a way of living.

"Men help each other by their joy," Ruskin said, "not by their sorrow." Sorrow may be the plow and the harrow which dig the soil and crumble it fine, but it is the fresh-springing plant of joy that is directly of benefit to our fellows. True it is that sorrow and joy are bound together and part of the same whole, but sorrow is for the inward side, joy for the outward. Aubrey de Vere wrote:

Grief should be
Like joy, majestic, equable, sedate;
Confirming, cleansing, raising, making free;
Strong to consume small troubles; to command
Great thoughts, grave thoughts, thoughts lasting
    to the end.

That is what we long to find in sorrow, something that makes us stronger and better for the experience; but as so often happens, the poet presents the desirable end without suggesting any way to achieve it. The realization to which William Penn attained, that they who live and love in the Omnipresent are never separated, suggests one way.

We thank thee for the dear and faithful dead, for those who have made the distant heavens a Home for us, and whose truth and beauty are even now in our hearts. One by one thou dost gather the scattered families out of the earthly light into the heavenly glory, from the distractions and strife and weariness of time to the peace of eternity. We thank thee for the labors and the joys of these mortal years, we thank thee for our deep sense of the mysteries that lie beyond our dust and for the eye of faith that thou hast opened for all who believe in thy Son to outlook that mark. May we live together in thy faith and love and in that hope which is full of immortality.

RUFUS ELLIS

PRAYERS FOR the dead went out of Protestant practice with the prayer book of 1549 and the Thirty-nine Articles of Faith. The picture Dante paints of weary souls released from years of toil in Purgatory through the masses paid for by their friends on earth is repugnant to us, both because of the somewhat commercial flavor of the transaction and because Purgatory itself has been discarded. But having thrown out these "blasphemous fables and dangerous deceits," we have tended also to thrust our beloved dead out of our religious exercises. Halloween is celebrated as the secular holiday perhaps most enjoyed by children of all of the holidays, but All Saints' Day, to which historically it was the prelude, is almost forgotten.

From its earliest days the Christian church has been remembering its saints and martyrs once a year, and from 835 the day has been fixed as November 1. From 998 until the Reformation, All Souls' Day followed on November 2, when the ordinary run of faithful departed were lovingly celebrated. The Protestants laid this aside, objecting to such grades and distinctions on the ground that in the New Testament the word "saints" was used for all the people of God who were sanctified by the Spirit. A service is appointed in the *Book of Common Prayer* for All Saints' Day as one of the major festivals of the church, but apart from devout Episcopalians, few people think, or even know, of it.

The traditional prayers for All Saints' Day refer to the cloud of witnesses by which we are surrounded and to the example of virtue which they offer us, remind us of their unseen fellowship as we run the race that is set before us, and point forward to the joys of heaven at the end. It is a noble concept. We have gained much by dropping the paid masses and emphasizing the communion of saints, but we have lost much too. We have lost intimacy and the opportunity, so comforting to us and so psychologically sound, to do something to help those whose passing has left such an aching emptiness behind. The dear, charming, human sinners have become a cloud of witnesses and models of virtue, to whom our prayers are useless.

In Japan, and in China too, of course, from where Japan took the custom, a three-day festival of the dead is held annually. It is a joyous time when the souls of the departed return to visit their families on earth. The living do everything in their power to make the visit a happy one. They provide food, little piles of vegetables on the sides of bridges, or formal services in the temples (paid for by the families) called Feeding the Hungry Ghosts. They provide entertainment. In one of Tokyo's great shrines I saw a beautiful display of flower arrangements set out for the pleasure of the unseen visitors. In a mountain village children made and decorated lanterns set on wheels, and at nightfall down all the little lanes came toddlers pulling lighted lanterns to the graves beside the temple.

Everywhere for three nights there is dancing before the local shrine. In wide circles, sometimes one inside another, the people of the neighborhood join in the Bon Odori, a folk dance for this occasion only. All ages are represented, young men with towels tied round their heads, young girls in gay kimonos, their long sleeves swaying to their graceful movements; old women, gray, wrinkled, skilled; tiny children, absorbed, jubilant, imitative.

Before the war and the shortages, when there were plenty of candles, those who lived by running streams sent their guests away at the end of the time in tiny boats, each with a lighted candle. They slipped down the river together, a fleet of little lights glimmering away into the dark.

Only simple and literal-minded people believe all of this, of course; most take it as we take our Christmas customs, for the sake of the love and joy and the poignant beauty of the symbolism; but it must warm hearts chilled by loneliness and separation and brighten memories grown dim.

Religious belief in the modern world has lost most of its old certainty of heaven. It was the story of the Resurrection, as someone has said, that made Christianity spread like wildfire around the basin of the Mediterranean. When in 627 the Roman abbot Paulinus went to England to preach the gospel, the Northumbrians said to him,

So seems the life of man as a sparrow's flight through the hall when you are sitting at meat in winter-tide, with the warm fire lighted on the hearth, but the icy rain-storm without. The sparrow flies in at one door and tarries for a moment in the light and heat of the hearthfire, and then flying forth from the other vanishes into the wintry darkness whence it came. So tarries for a moment the life of man in our sight, but what is before it, what after it, we know not. If this new teaching tell us aught certainly of these, let us follow it.

Now, however, we say little about the life of the world to come, stressing instead the teachings of Jesus and their bearing on social justice. Perhaps it is more true, as well as more humble, to admit that we cannot know with certainty what lies beyond the horizon, to accept, in Wordsworth's phrase, the burden of the mystery. But the night has stars and universes of light in comparison with which the hearth fire in the hall is dim and smoky and brief as a candle's flame.

This prayer of Rufus Ellis, an English minister of the past century, reminds us to give joyous thanks for our beloved dead. Though there is nothing we can do for them, we can remember gratefully all they have done for us, and been to us, not only in their high moments but in the sweet familiar homely ones. Thankful too we must be for the experience of continuing companionship that comes to us at times, and the deep conviction that beyond the separation and the mystery we shall find one another once again in God.

I HAVE WRITTEN of the sense that one has from time to time of the continuing companionship of the beloved dead. This is not a matter of intellectual theory or belief to me, but of experience. I have never consciously sought it; I do not receive messages from beyond or attend seances, for I have always thought that in whatever life the dead may go on to beyond this one, they have something much better to do than to linger on our outskirts waiting for a medium to summon them. But there have been times, when I was alone in a scene of great natural beauty, when I have been aware of the presence of one whom I loved and could not see. The joy of the moment and the lasting, vivid quality of the memory seem to speak for its authenticity.

In some very inadequate lines I have attempted to write of one such experience, typical of all. In England in the spring, I had a strong feeling that I must go to Ewelme, of which I knew only that it was an old village in a corner of Oxfordshire which Chaucer visited and where his son and granddaughter were buried. It can be reached by bus from Oxford,

but the weather was too bad while I was there
and so I had to make a more complicated trip
from Jordans in Buckinghamshire.  I set off
alone one morning, took a train to Princes
Risborough, suppressing the temptation to
find the Pink and Lily Inn which Rupert Brooke
loved, took another train, so small that it was
toylike, to Watlington, and from there walked
five or six miles over the Chiltern Hills.  That
walk, which I shall never forget, I have tried to
describe in these lines:

### The Road to Ewelme

I was alone on that road.
Clouds moved swiftly overhead,
And a light as clear as water
Lay on the horizon.  It was May,
The hawthorn white with bloom,
Saint Mary's lace wincing in the wind
Beside the road.  A lapwing cried,
Soaring and dipping above the field
Where rabbits huddles in circles,
Brown and bowed their small bodies.

Drenched by sudden rain that swept
Like dim curtains blowing,
I walked toward Ewelme, where
Chaucer's son lay buried,
Where in five centuries the feet of old men

Have hollowed the stone steps between
The almshouse and the church.

I walked alone, wind-buffeted
Feeling the chill fingers of rain
Touch my face, tasting the rain
On my lips, hearing the lapwing's cry,
Smelling the wet, warm earth,
Seeing the storm move toward the world's edge
And the pale sun run after it.
I walked alone in that wide country.

Yet not alone.  Oh, not alone!
And I, who hold the dead do not
Return to the living, being free,
Not hovering nostalgic over old scenes,
Not bound even by old loves,
I sang aloud on the empty road,
Exulting, rich at heart, because
You walked there with me.

He who binds to himself a joy
Doth the winged life destroy
But he who kisses a joy as it flies
Lives in eternity's sunrise.

WILLIAM BLAKE

IN THE USUAL version the word "binds" is given
as "bends," but Gerald Bullitt, including this
quatrain of Blake's in his anthology, *Testament
of Light,* makes a good case for the reading
"binds," and that is the form in which I have
chosen to remember it.

There are a thousand ways, I suppose, in
which Christ's great truth, "Whosoever shall
seek to save his life shall lose it, and whosoever
shall lose his life shall preserve it," has been
paraphrased, but this of Blake's is, I think, one
of the most beautiful.

"Above all the grace and the gifts that Christ
gives to His beloved," said St. Francis of Assisi,
"is that of overcoming self." Surely one of the

most effective and most necessary ways of overcoming self is that of learning not to lay one's hot, possessive hands on the joys that one values, whether the winged life be that of natural beauty, of human affection, or even that of spiritual growth. The fourteenth-century author of *The Cloud of Unknowing*, that most original of anonymous mystics who wrote of meditation and contemplation as Chaucer might have done, with humor and humanity and perfection of style, sees danger even in fastening oneself too eagerly and possessively on the joys that come from meditation and the practice of the presence of God. "Be wary in this work, and strain not thine heart rudely nor out of measure; but work more with a list than with any worthless strength," he said, ". . . and snatch not overhastily as it were a greedy greyhound, hunger thee never so sore."

O Lord, I know not what I ought to ask of thee; thou only knowest what I need; thou lovest me better than I know how to love myself. O Father! give to thy child that which he himself knows not how to ask. I dare not ask either for crosses or consolations; I simply present myself before thee, I open my heart to thee. Behold my needs which I know not myself; see and do according to thy mercy. Smite or heal, depress me or raise me up; I adore all thy purposes without knowing them; I am silent; I offer myself in sacrifice; I yield myself to thee; I would have no other desire than to accomplish thy will. Teach me to pray. Pray thyself in me.

FRANÇOIS DE LA MOTHE FÉNELON

❧❦❧

THIS SEEMS to me the prayer of perfect commitment, of the complete yielding of one's own will to the divine will and even of one's own ideas of one's own needs. A long prayer and a profound one, packed with thought as well as feeling, it might well be broken up and prayed in parts, at different times.

It is not an easy prayer to make sincerely. Most of us think that we know pretty well what we want and need, and silence in the inward heart is even more difficult to achieve than silence of the tongue. I saw this prayer once included in a collection of prayers, and in the margin beside the words, "Depress me or raise me up," some honest, outraged hand had written, "Oh, *no!!*" Honesty in prayer is the primary and basic essential, and if what we really want is *not* to be depressed, then we must certainly omit that clause. But still we can say, "I present myself before thee." We can alter the prayer if necessary, and say, "I wish to yield myself to thee." Dom John Chapman, the abbot of Downside, in England, who, according to Evelyn Underhill, knew more about prayer than anyone else she knew, wrote: "It is not necessary to 'want God and want nothing else.' You have only to 'want to want God and want to want nothing else.' Few get beyond this really."

François de la Mothe Fénelon, Archbishop of Cambrai, who lived from 1651 to 1715, just within the span of William Penn's life, is best known as the spiritual advisor to Madame de Maintenon and other highly placed French women. His letters of spiritual counsel have become religious classics. Two of his books have been issued in a fine modern translation by Mildred Whitney Stillman under the titles *Christian Perfection* and *Spiritual Letters of Fénelon*.

It is less well known that he was for five years the tutor to the Duke of Burgundy, who was the eldest grandson of Louis XIV and who would have succeeded to the throne of France if he had lived. During his formative years, the boy's "violent, haughty, and passionate character" was softened and tendered by the influence and wise guidance of his mentor Fénelon. The *Catholic Encyclopedia* even hints that Fénelon succeeded too well in taming his pupil. After Fénelon retired from the court to his abbey of St. Valéry, he continued his correspondence with the Duke of Burgundy for some twenty years, until the young man's death in 1712.

Fénelon in his turn was guided by Madame Guyon, who, with Miguel de Molinos and Fénelon himself, was a leader of the Quietest movement, which had so much influence upon the Society of Friends. At the time of his appointment to the tutorship in 1689, she wrote to the thirty-eight-year-old Fénelon a long letter, of which this is a part:

When the moment of duty and of action comes, you may be assured that God will not fail to bestow upon you those dispositions and qualifications which are appropriate to the situation in which His providence has placed you. Act always without regard to *self.* The less you have of self, the more you will have of God."

One can see a reflection of these words in a statement of Fénelon's which came to be a source of strength to me when I was placed in a somewhat similar situation without the qualifications and dispositions which were his in such abundance. Short enough to be slipped through the mind in the few seconds before any "moment of duty and of action," this talisman sentence helps to release tension, to restore a sense of proportion, to distract one's attention away from the anxious and importunate self:

"Cheered by the presence of God, I will do each moment, without anxiety, according to the strength which He shall give me, the work that His Providence assigns me."

# NIGHT

The sun descending in the west,
    The evening star does shine;
The birds are silent in their nest,
    And I must seek for mine.
        The moon, like a flower
        In heaven's high bower,
        With silent delight
        Sits and smiles on the night.

Farewell, green fields and happy grove,
    Where flocks have took delight:
Where lambs have nibbled, silent move
    The feet of angels bright;
        Unseen they pour blessing
        And joy without ceasing
        On each bud and blossom,
        On each sleeping bosom.

They look in every thoughtless nest
    Where birds are covered warm;
They visit caves of every beast,
    To keep them all from harm:
        If they see any weeping
        That should have been sleeping,
        They pour sleep on their head,
        And sit down by their bed.

Where wolves and tigers howl for prey,
    They pitying stand and weep,
Seeking to drive their thirst away
    And keep them from the sheep.
        But if they rush dreadful,
        The angels, most heedful,
        Receive each mild spirit,
        New worlds to inherit.

And there the lion's ruddy eyes
    Shall flow with tears of gold:
And pitying the tender cries,
    And walking round the fold:
        Saying, "Wrath by His meekness,
        And, by His health, sickness,
        Are driven away
        From our immortal day.

"And now beside thee, bleating lamb,
    I can lie down and sleep,
Or think on Him who bore thy name,
    Graze after thee, and weep.
        For, wash'd in life's river,
        My bright mane for ever
        Shall shine like the gold
        As I guard o'er the fold."

WILLIAM BLAKE

WILLIAM BLAKE'S *Songs of Innocence* has been called "unquestionably one of the most perfectly beautiful books of the world," both because of its format, each exquisite page designed and engraved by Blake himself, and because of the poems in it. Published in 1789, when the French Revolution was raging, when reason was god in the intellectual world and the influence of Pope and Dryden held English poetry in a vise, when melancholy was a cult and enthusiasm a disgrace, this book of poems was as revolutionary and as significant as the first snow-drop that pushes its head through the frost-hard ground. The seeds of the Romantic Movement were being tended in the poetic greenhouses, but Blake's blossom was a wildflower in the winter forest.

One of the loveliest of the songs is this called "Night." Its theme is, of course, the problem of evil in nature: why do the strong prey on the weak, and the lion and the lamb lie down together only "in our immortal day"? It suggests that the night of this earthly world is the preparation for the day of eternity and that after being "wash'd in the river of life" the lion of evil becomes a force for good, his mane shining gold and glorious as he guards the lambs which once he would have devoured.

Yet even into the night come messengers from the day, and the soul seeking its rest is watched over by bright angels from the eternal.

The *Songs of Innocence,* according to S. Foster Damon, who has written one of the best and most scholarly books on Blake, deal not only with the innocence of childhood and inexperience, but with the mystical state of illumination, when the eyes of the spirit are first opened, when eternity is made "manifest in the light of day," and the whole world has, as George Fox said, "a new smell." There is over all these poems, which are written with a limpidity and simplicity that seems artless but is the product of the highest technical skill, an unearthly and ineffable shine. They produce with words the same effect that Blake got in his painting of the "Infant Jesus at Prayer." No one who has seen that picture can ever forget the light, the tenderness, the unearthly glory that seem to emanate from it in a sort of delicate shining and breathing.

Whether or not you find in the *Songs of Innocence* the deeper meanings that may be there, you cannot escape the impact of the poetic emotion that they embody. A. E. Housman, author of *The Shropshire Lad* and no mystic, wrote in his *Name and Nature of Poetry:*

121

"Blake again and again, as Shakespeare now and then, gives us poetry neat or adulterated with so little meaning that nothing except poetic emotion is perceived or matters." I don't know whether he would have included "Night" among his examples of poetry neat, or not, but I think it could be read that way and still not lose its power. Indeed, I think that often this is the truest way to read poetry, delighting in the magic of its images and cadences, allowing the active analytic surface mind to cease its restless questioning, and the deep-self, which understands symbols without translating them, to receive the full substance of the poem and be made richer by it. People sometimes believe themselves to be defeated by poetry because they do not understand it, whereas often the poet's intention is most successfully grasped by the reader when the poem is not understood, but felt.

"O God," I said, and that was all. But what are the prayers of the whole universe more than expansions of that one cry? It is not what God can give us, but God that we want.

GEORGE MacDONALD

MEAN HIMSELF and none of His goods," the author of the *Cloud of Unknowing* had said five centuries earlier. None of His goods, not courage to do His work, nor joy to share with others, not even the quiet mind. God himself.

The modern Irish poet and novelist, James Stephens, has put the same thought into verse:

> Do never pray
> But only say
> O Thou!
>
> And leave it so,
> For He will know
> —Somehow—
>
> That you fall,
> And that you call
> On Him now.

THERE ARE many ways to pray, and each soul must find its own. The important, the essential thing, is to pray.

"I started with a disbelief in God and prayer," wrote Gandhi in *The Cultural World,* "and until a late stage in life I did not feel anything like a void in life. At that stage I felt that as food was indispensable to the body, so was prayer indispensable for the soul. . . . I am not a man of learning, but I do humbly claim to be a man of prayer. I am indifferent to the form. Everyone is a law unto himself."

And Dom John Chapman wrote to "one living in the world," "Pray as you can, don't try to pray as you can't." And again, "The only way to pray is to pray, and the way to pray well is to pray much."

THE FINAL POEM is said to have been written on the morning of the day on which Emily Brontë used her pencil and put it aside for the last time. There is probably no genius in all of English literature so mysterious as the genius of Emily Brontë. In her short span of thirty years, she wrote perhaps the greatest and certainly the most original novel in the language and a number of poems that will not die. Though her life for most of those thirty years was enclosed in the lonely moorland parish of her birth, her mind, wild and passionate and free, soared into remote regions beyond thought and experience and found there truth. Her genius broke through her talent for expression as a powerful engine shakes and jars the light body of a car.

This statement of faith in the God within invites and indeed endures no comment. In his *Creed of Christ* Gerald Heard speaks of the modern tendency to create God out of our own mild feelings of "humanitarianism and uplift whereby we get on with our friends and plan for the poor," as the sin against the Holy Ghost. These "Last Lines" of Emily Brontë's describe

a God who is the antithesis of that mild creation
out of our self-complacency: the God of
Supreme Reality and Power, yet heart of our
heart and breath of our breath.

No coward soul is mine,
No trembler in the world's storm-troubled sphere:
    I see Heaven's glories shine,
And faith shines equal, arming me from fear.

    O God within my breast,
Almighty, ever-present Deity!
    Life—that in me has rest,
As I—undying Life—have power in Thee!

    Vain are the thousand creeds
That move men's hearts: unutterably vain;
    Worthless as wither'd weeds,
Or idlest froth amid the boundless main,

    To waken doubt in one
Holding so fast by Thine Infinity;
    So surely anchor'd on
The steadfast rock of immortality.

    With wide-embracing love
Thy Spirit animates eternal years,

Pervades and broods above,
Changes, sustains, dissolves, creates, and rears.

Though earth and man were gone,
And suns and universes ceased to be,
And Thou wert left alone,
Every existence would exist in Thee.

There is not room for Death,
Nor atom that his might could render void:
Thou—Thou art Being and Breath,
And what Thou art may never be destroyed.

EMILY BRONTË